"That's the last," said the man
as he put Mag in the box.
"That's the last," said the man
as he closed the lid.

"That's the last," said the man as he loaded the truck.

The truck drove off.
Mag lifted the lid and looked out.
"Where am I?" he said.
"I'm supposed to be going to school."

Just then the truck
went over a big bump
and CLANG
Mag fell out onto the road.

"Oh" cried Mag.
"Where am I?
I'm supposed to be going to school."
"School" said the dog.
"I know where the school is.
Stick to me and I'll take you there."
And off he ran.

Mag tried to stick to the dog
but he couldn't.
So he ran after
him as fast as he could,
shouting "Stick to me!"

The dog disappeared into the park.
"Stick to me please" shouted Mag
– and some things did and some didn't.

"That's strange" said Mag. "I wonder why."

The dog disappeared
round behind the dustbins.
"Stick to me," shouted Mag
– and some things did
and some didn't.

"That's strange," said Mag.
"I wonder why."

The dog went
in through someone's back door,
and out at the front.
"Stick to me," shouted Mag
– and some things did
and some didn't.

"That's strange," said Mag.
"I wonder why."

The dog stopped
by the school gate.
"Here you are," he said.

"All you had to do
was stick to me."
Mag stopped to rest.
"I tried to stick to
you," said Mag. "You went too fast for me, but

some things have stuck to me
and I don't know why."

“I wish someone could tell me why.”

“We can tell you
and we can show you,”
said the children.

And they did.